LET'S LEARN ABOUT
COMPUTER SCIENCE

SOFTWARE

Jeff Mapua

Enslow Publishing
101 W. 23rd Street
Suite 240
New York, NY 10011
USA

enslow.com

WORDS TO KNOW

application software A program or group of programs that help a computer do a task.

bug A mistake that makes a program fail.

data Information that is used in a computer.

hardware The parts of a computer that you can touch.

operating system Software that allows all of the computer programs to work.

program Step-by-step instructions that tell a computer what to do with data.

programming software A computer program used to make, fix, or help other software.

software The programs used by a computer.

system software The software that helps the computer run.

task A job.

upgrade A change to software that makes it better.

CONTENTS

**A smartphone
needs software
to do its job.**

What Is Software?

Have you ever used a computer or a smartphone? If so, then you have used **software**. Software means the instructions a computer follows. **Programs** are software.

Fast Fact

The word "software" was first used in the 1960s.

Hardware means the parts of the computer you can touch—both inside and out.

Software vs. Hardware

Computer **hardware** is the parts of a computer you can touch. A keyboard is hardware. Software is the parts of a computer you cannot touch. You use a computer to run software.

FAST FACT

Software was first saved on stiff paper cards with holes punched in them.

Each kind of software allows a computer to do different tasks.

Types of Software

There are different types of software. The three main types are **system software**, **programming software**, and **application software**. Each kind helps people do different things.

The operating system on your computer helps run all of its programs.

System Software

System software helps computers run. The **operating system** is system software. It controls how the computer works. It helps run programs. It also works with hardware, like printers.

FAST FACT

Popular operating systems include Windows, Mac OS, and Linux.

Computer code is written in a way that computers understand.

Programming Software

Programming software helps people write programs. It helps them write instructions that a computer can understand. It also helps fix broken software.

FAST FACT

Programming software includes tools called compilers, editors, and interpreters.

You could not play games on your computer without software!

Application Software

Application software is used to do a **task**. It can be one program or a group of small programs. Computer games are a kind of application software.

Fast Fact

An "app" on your computer is short for "application."

Sometimes people go to a computer store to get an upgrade. It helps their computer to run better.

Upgrades

Software can change. Sometimes operating systems get **upgrades**. These upgrades can fix a problem. Upgrades can also make computer security better.

FAST FACT

Software can be deleted forever.

You can share software on your computer, just like sharing a pizza with your friends.

Sharing

Computer software can be shared with others. Software is **data** saved on a computer. This data can be copied. Those copies can be shared.

Fast Fact

Napster made sharing music files popular in the late 1990s.

Having bugs on your computer can harm your software. It is important to get it fixed quickly.

Bugs

Software can have errors. These are called **bugs**. Bugs can make software break or give strange results. Fixing a bug is called debugging. Bugs can cause big problems if they are left alone.

Fast Fact

The Y2K bug was a date error where software read the year 2000 as 1900.

Activity
Fun with Software

MATERIALS

paper
pencil
computer

Here are some ways to learn more about software:

Get to know a word processor software.

Write a letter on paper to a friend or family member. Then type the letter into a word processor on a computer or mobile device. Popular word processors include Microsoft Word, Notepad, and Google Docs.

Learn how to perform operating system tasks with the help of an adult! On a computer, create a file. It could be a new letter, an image, a sound file, or anything you can think of. Copy the file and paste the copy of the file. Then delete the copy of the file you made.

LEARN MORE

Books

Gifford, Clive. *Amazing Applications and Perfect Programs*. New York, NY: Crabtree, 2015.

Liukas, Linda. *Hello Ruby: Journey Inside the Computer*. New York, NY: Feiwel & Friends, 2017.

Small, Cathleen. *What Are Hardware and Software?* New York, NY: Britannica, 2017.

Websites

Fisher-Price Games & Activities

play.fisher-price.com / en_US / GamesandActivities / play-and-learn-activities / index.html

Check out these fun games and activities to play and learn more about how to use a computer!

PBS Kids

pbskids.org

Learn how to use a computer with these fun games online. Find and download fun apps to play.

INDEX

Published in 2019 by Enslow Publishing, LLC.
101 W. 23rd Street, Suite 240, New York, NY 10011

Copyright © 2019 by Enslow Publishing, LLC.

Library of Congress Cataloging-in-Publication Data

Names: Mapua, Jeff, author.

Title: Software / Jeff Mapua.

Description: New York, NY : Enslow Publishing, LLC., 2019. | Series: Let's learn about computer science | Includes bibliographical references and index. | Audience: Grades K to 4.

Identifiers: LCCN 2018005415| ISBN 9781978501805 (library bound) | ISBN 9781978502338 (pbk.) | ISBN 9781978502345 (6 pack)

Subjects: LCSH: Computer software—Juvenile literature.

Classification: LCC QA76.754 .M365 2019 | DDC 005.3—dc23

LC record available at https://lccn.loc.gov/2018005415

Printed in the United States of America

To Our Readers: We have done our best to make sure all website addresses in this book were active and appropriate when we went to press. However, the author and the publisher have no control over and assume no liability for the material available on those websites or on any websites they may link to. Any comments or suggestions can be sent by e-mail to customerservice@enslow.com.

Photos Credits: Cover, p. 1 KidStock/Blend Images/Getty Images; pp. 2, 3, 24 Best-Backgrounds/Shutterstock.com; p. 4 Maridav/Shutterstock.com; p. 6 Ljupco Smokovski/Shutterstock.com; p. 8 Wayhome studio/Shutterstock.com; p. 10 RoSonic/Shutterstock.com; p. 12 patpitchaya/Shutterstock.com; p. 14 BestPhotoStudio/Shutterstock.com; p. 16 Gorodenkoff/Shutterstock.com; p. 18 Monkey Business Images/Shutterstock.com; p. 20 fizkes/Shutterstock.com; p. 22 jamesteohart/Shutterstock.com; interior design elements (laptop) ArthurStock/Shutterstock.com, (flat screen computer) Aleksandrs Bondars/Shutterstock.com.